P
636.9322
-Coo-

RABBITS

BARNYARD FRIENDS

Jason Cooper

The Rourke Book Co., Inc.
Vero Beach, Florida 32964

© 1995 The Rourke Book Co., Inc.

All rights reserved. No part of this book may be reproduced or utilized in any form or by any means, electronic or mechanical including photocopying, recording or by any information storage and retrieval system without permission in writing from the publisher.

Edited by Sandra A. Robinson and Pamela J.P. Schroeder

PHOTO CREDITS
All photos © Lynn M. Stone

Library of Congress Cataloging-in-Publication Data

Cooper, Jason, 1942-
   Rabbits / by Jason Cooper.
   p. cm. — (Barn yard friends)
   Includes index.
   ISBN 1-55916-090-X
   1. Rabbits—Juvenile literature. [1. Rabbits. 2. Farm life.]
I. Title. II. Series: Cooper, Jason, 1942- Barn yard friends.
SF453.2.C65   1995
636'.9322—dc20   94-39533
                                                           CIP
                                                           AC

3 5944 00067 8977

Printed in the USA

TABLE OF CONTENTS

Rabbits	5
How Rabbits Look	6
Where Rabbits Live	9
Breeds of Rabbits	11
Wild Rabbits	14
Baby Rabbits	16
How Rabbits Are Raised	19
How Rabbits Act	20
How Rabbits Are Used	22
Glossary	23
Index	24

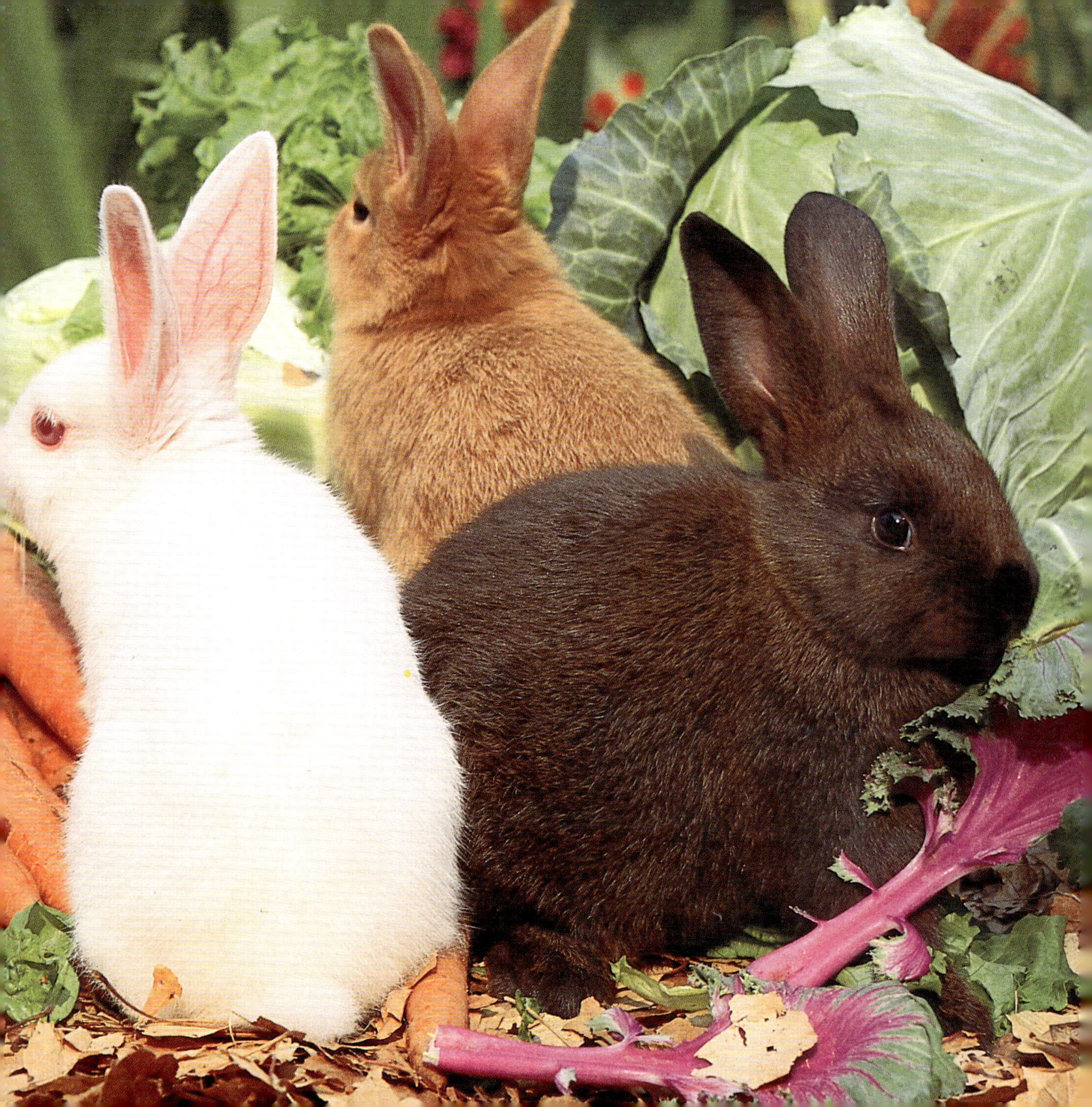

RABBITS

Wild rabbits *visit* farmers' gardens. **Domestic,** or tame, rabbits live their whole lives on the farm.

Some farmers raise a few domestic rabbits along with their other farm animals, such as sheep or cattle. Other farmers, known as rabbit **breeders,** only raise rabbits. Their rabbit farms are called **rabbitries.**

A rabbitry can be quite small. Several hundred rabbits can live in a garage-sized building.

Rabbit breeders raise bunnies in many colors and sizes

HOW RABBITS LOOK

Rabbits are soft, furry animals with long, strong hind legs. Rabbits have long ears and short "cotton puff" tails.

Domestic rabbits may be reddish, white, black, brown, gray or a mixture of colors.

Small **breeds,** or kinds, of rabbits weigh as little as two pounds. The biggest domestic rabbits weigh almost 20 pounds!

Some adult rabbits have a loose flap of skin called a dewlap under their throats.

The ears of lop rabbits, like this French lop, tilt down

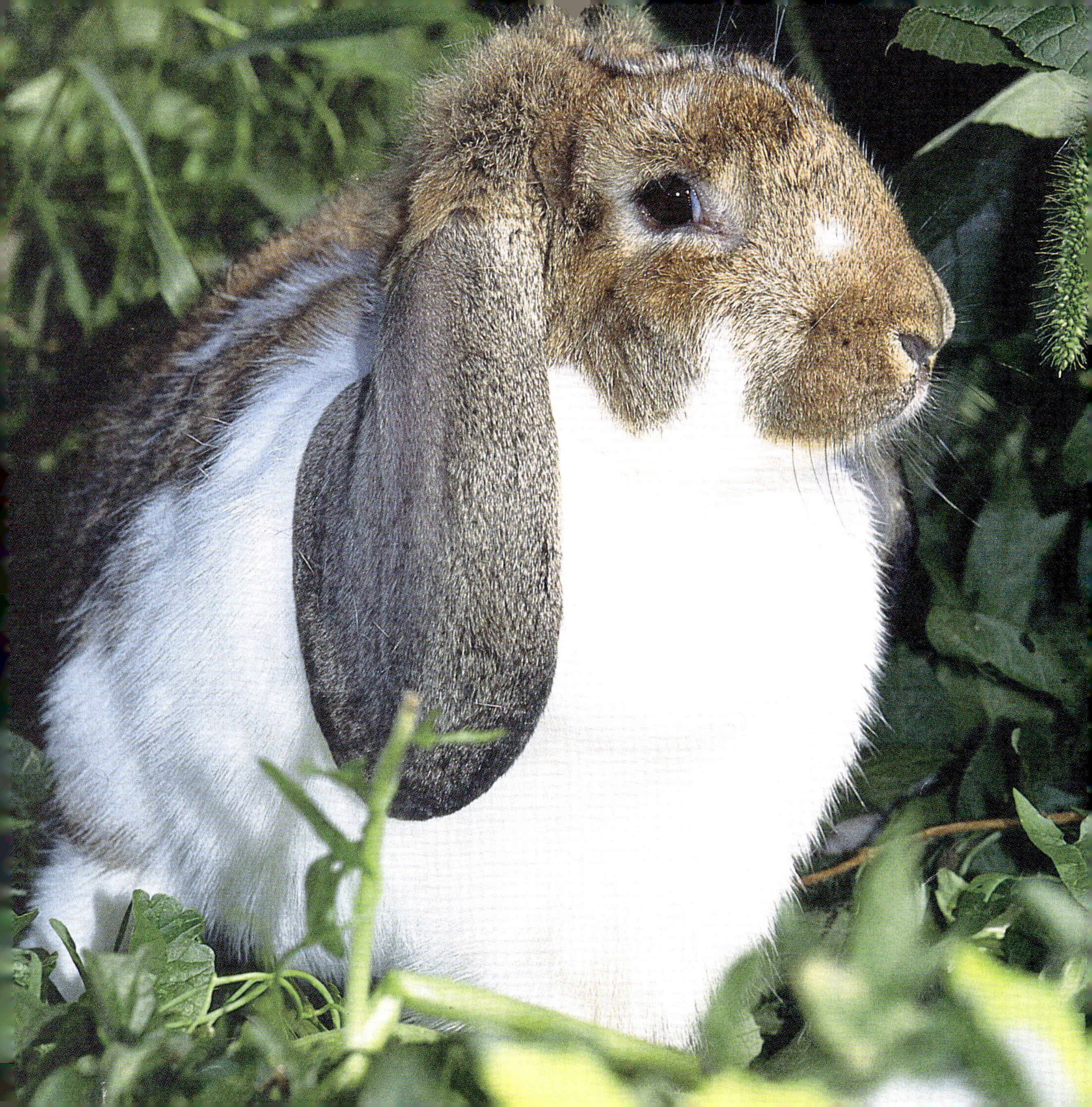

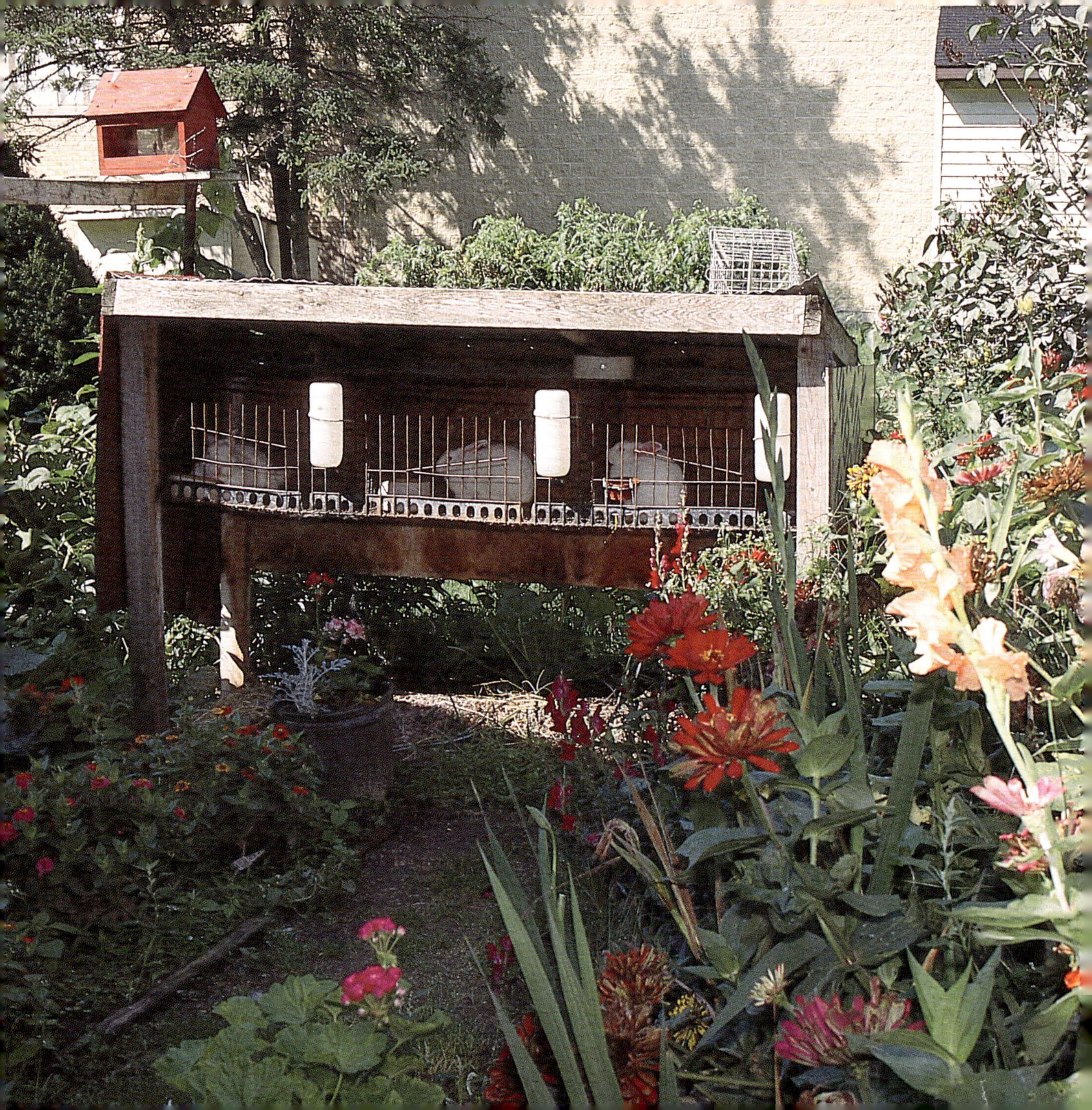

WHERE RABBITS LIVE

Rabbits are raised throughout North America and in many other parts of the world.

Rabbit farmers usually keep their rabbits in wire cages known as **hutches.** Hutches are often stacked upon each other like shelves. Stacked rabbit hutches look like rabbit apartment houses.

This outdoor hutch holds several white New Zealand breed rabbits

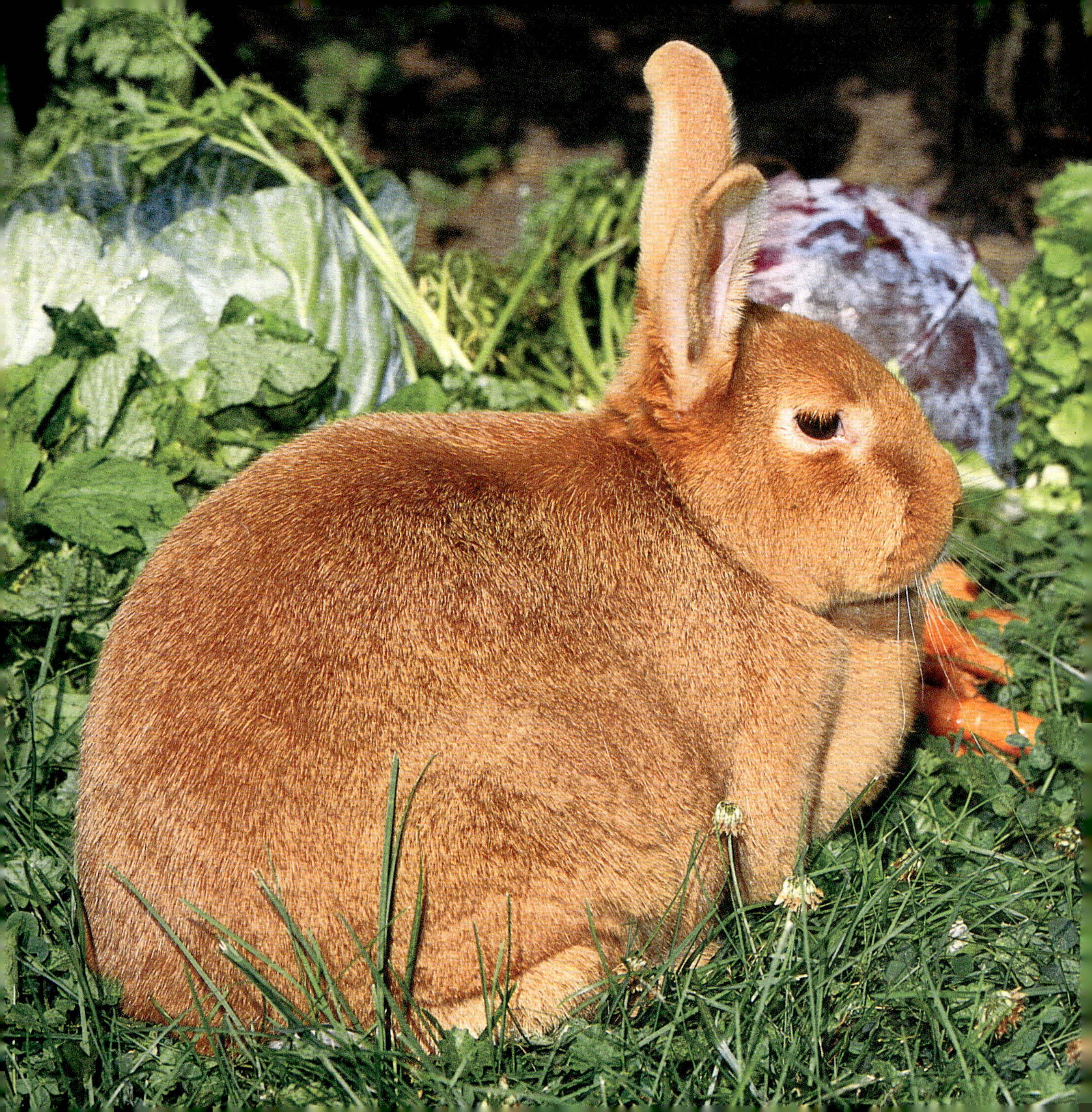

BREEDS OF RABBITS

Long ago, people in Europe caught wild rabbits and tamed them. These people were the first rabbit breeders.

Rabbit breeders choose which rabbits will be mothers and fathers. By choosing certain kinds of rabbits to be parents, breeders can control the size and color of rabbits.

Breeders now raise about 45 different domestic breeds. Each rabbit breed is different from the others in ear length, fur length, size and color.

New Zealand rabbits are one of the largest breeds

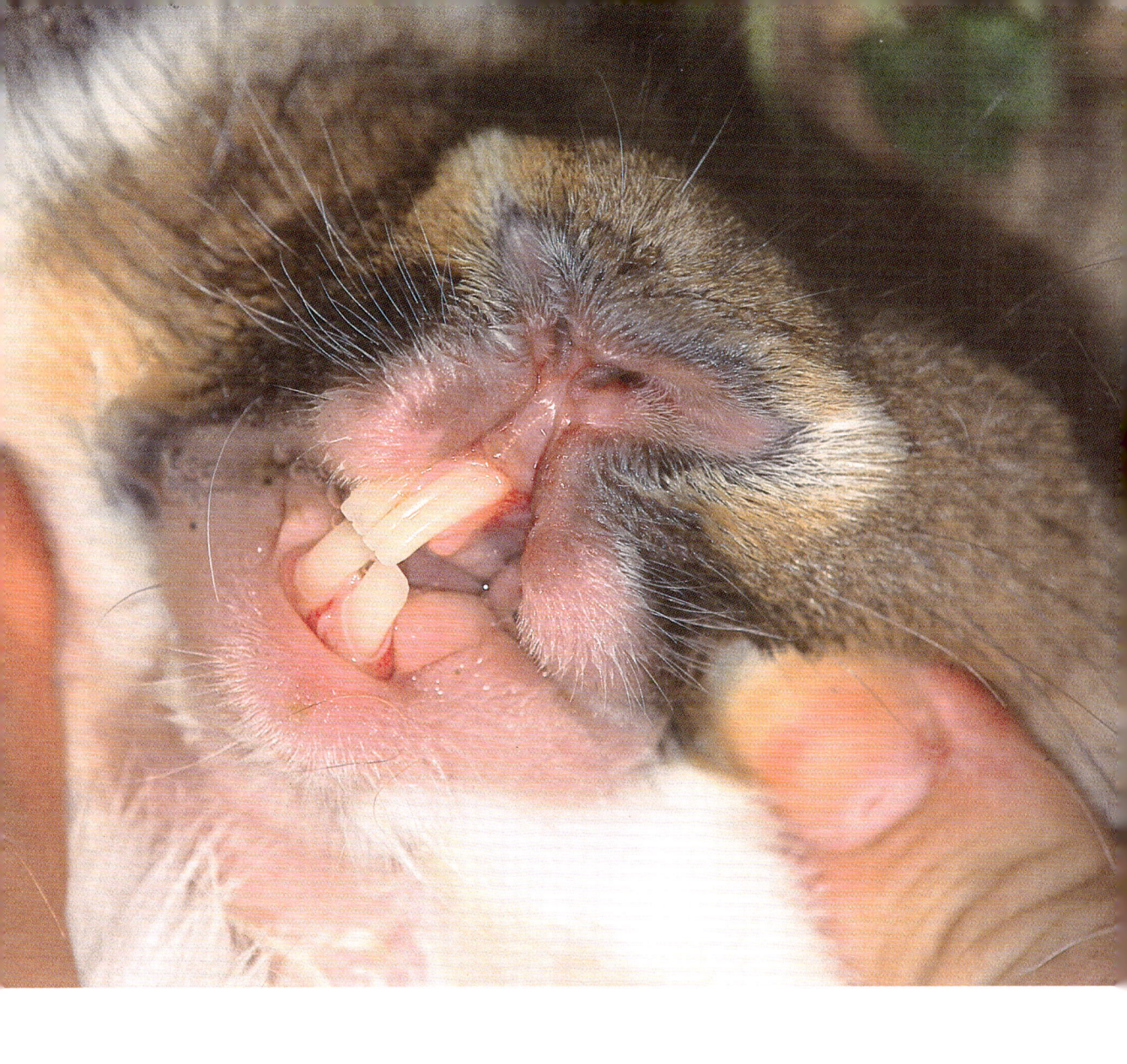

With help from a breeder, a rabbit shows off the front teeth that nibble so well

The Holland lop is a much smaller breed than the French lop

WILD RABBITS

Wild rabbits and hares live on every continent except Antarctica. They belong to a group of animals called **lagomorphs.**

Hares and rabbits are close cousins. Hares are generally larger than rabbits and have longer ears. Hares are more active at birth than rabbits.

The wild snowshoe and jack "rabbits" of North America are really hares. The most common North American wild rabbits are cottontails.

This wild snowshoe rabbit is really a hare, and it is sometimes called a varying hare

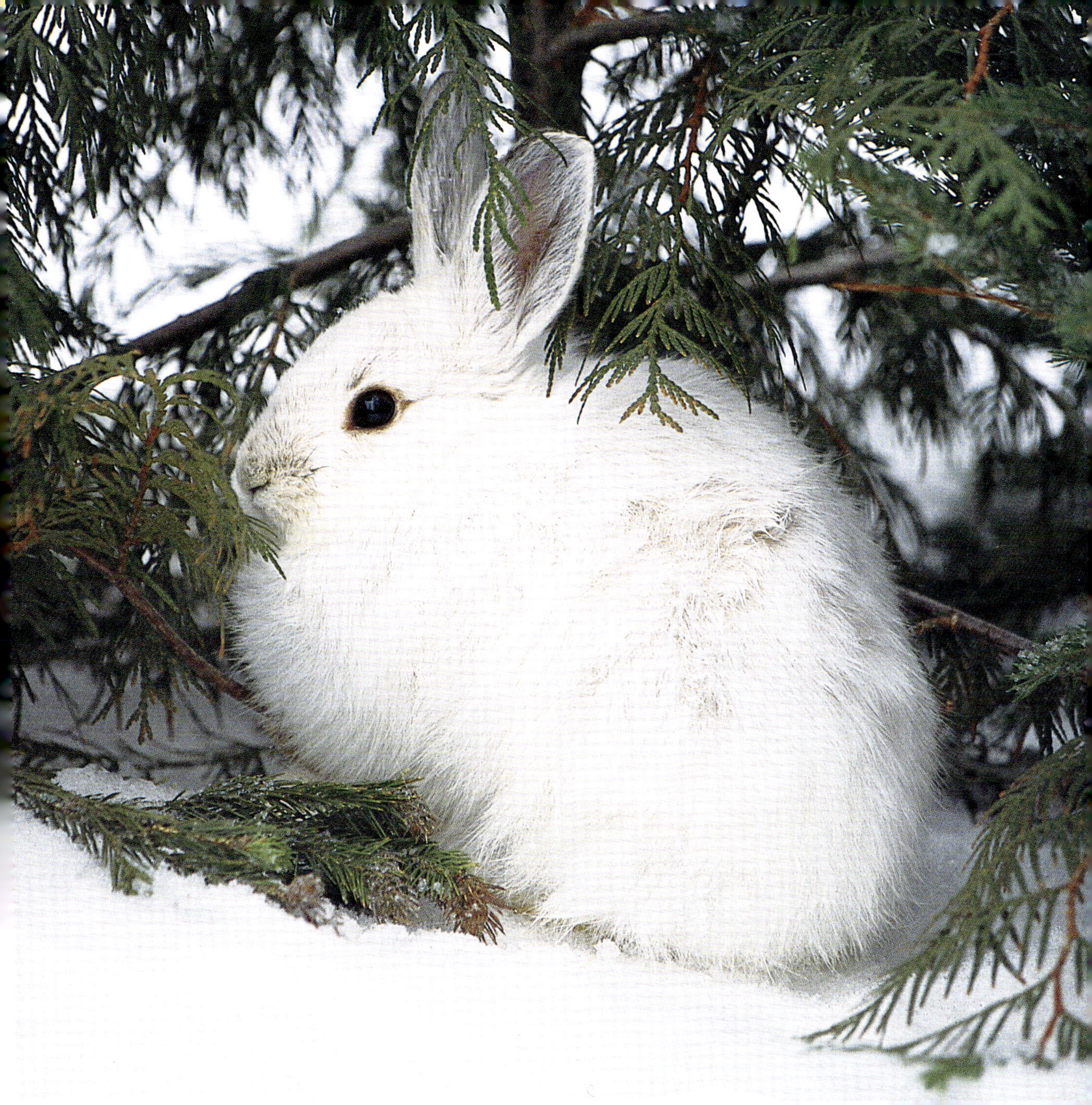

BABY RABBITS

Domestic rabbits have four or five **litters,** or groups of babies, each year. A litter is usually five or six babies, known as kits. Kits grow up quickly. By the time they are six months old, small-breed rabbits can begin their own families.

Domestic rabbits often live to be seven or eight years old.

These baby lops will not open their eyes until they are several days old

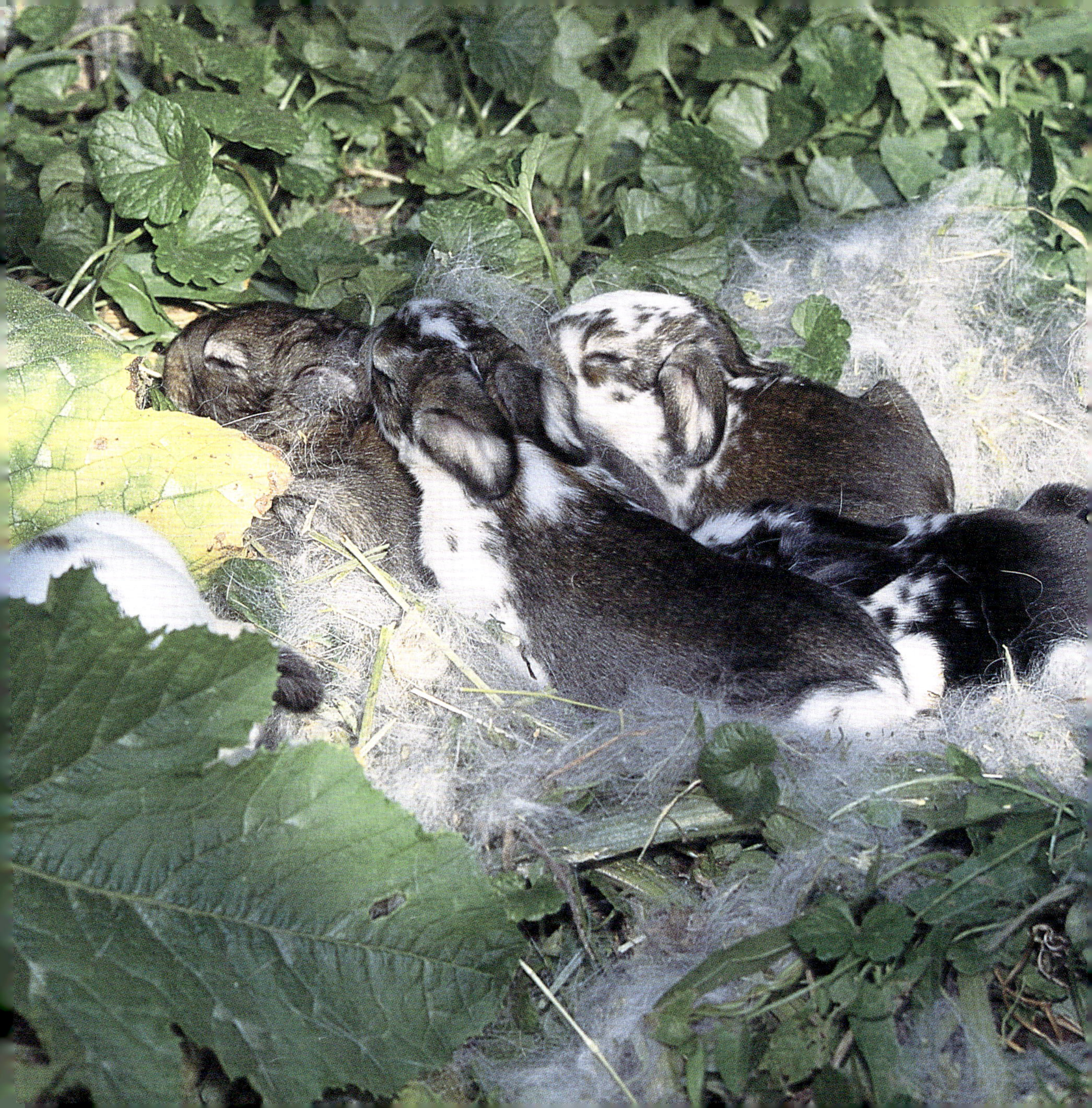

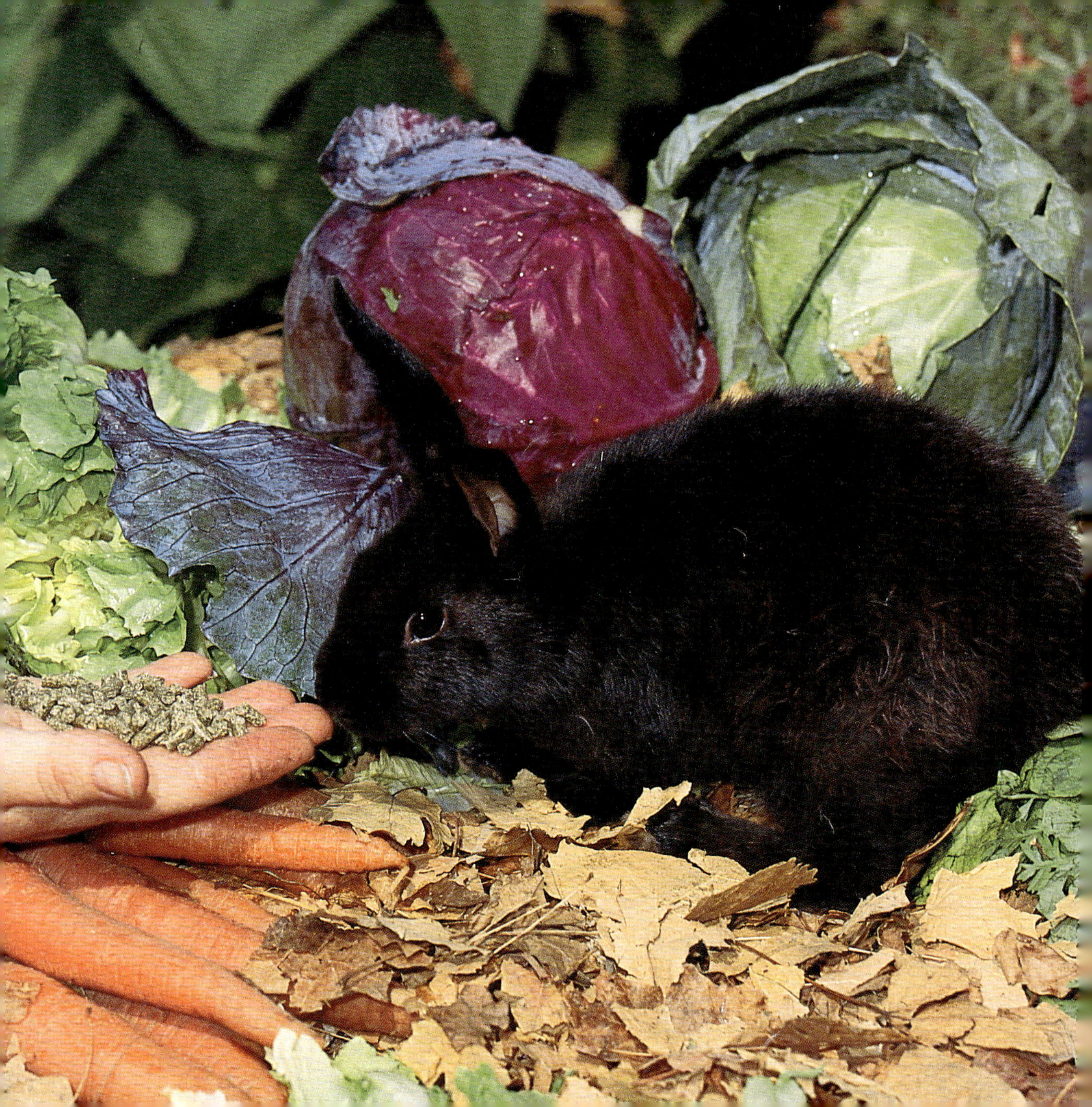

HOW RABBITS ARE RAISED

Wild rabbits feel right at home in vegetable gardens and pastures of clover.

Domestic rabbits rarely munch on fresh greens, and most wouldn't know a carrot from a caramel candy. That's because breeders feed their rabbits a strict diet of food pellets. Pellets contain a mixture of alfalfa, corn, vitamins and other healthy bunny foods.

Breeders sometimes treat their rabbits to greens, dandelions or maple leaves.

For most domestic rabbits, pellets make up the lion's share — most — of their diet

HOW RABBITS ACT

Domestic rabbits spend most of their lives in hutches where they eat, drink and sleep. They are calm, quiet and curious animals.

Wild rabbits are much more active than their domestic cousins. Wild rabbits always have to watch for enemies — dogs, foxes, bobcats and other hunting animals. When frightened, wild rabbits can hop along at nearly 20 miles per hour, and zigzag through trees and brush.

Out for exercise, a domestic rabbit hops through a pumpkin patch

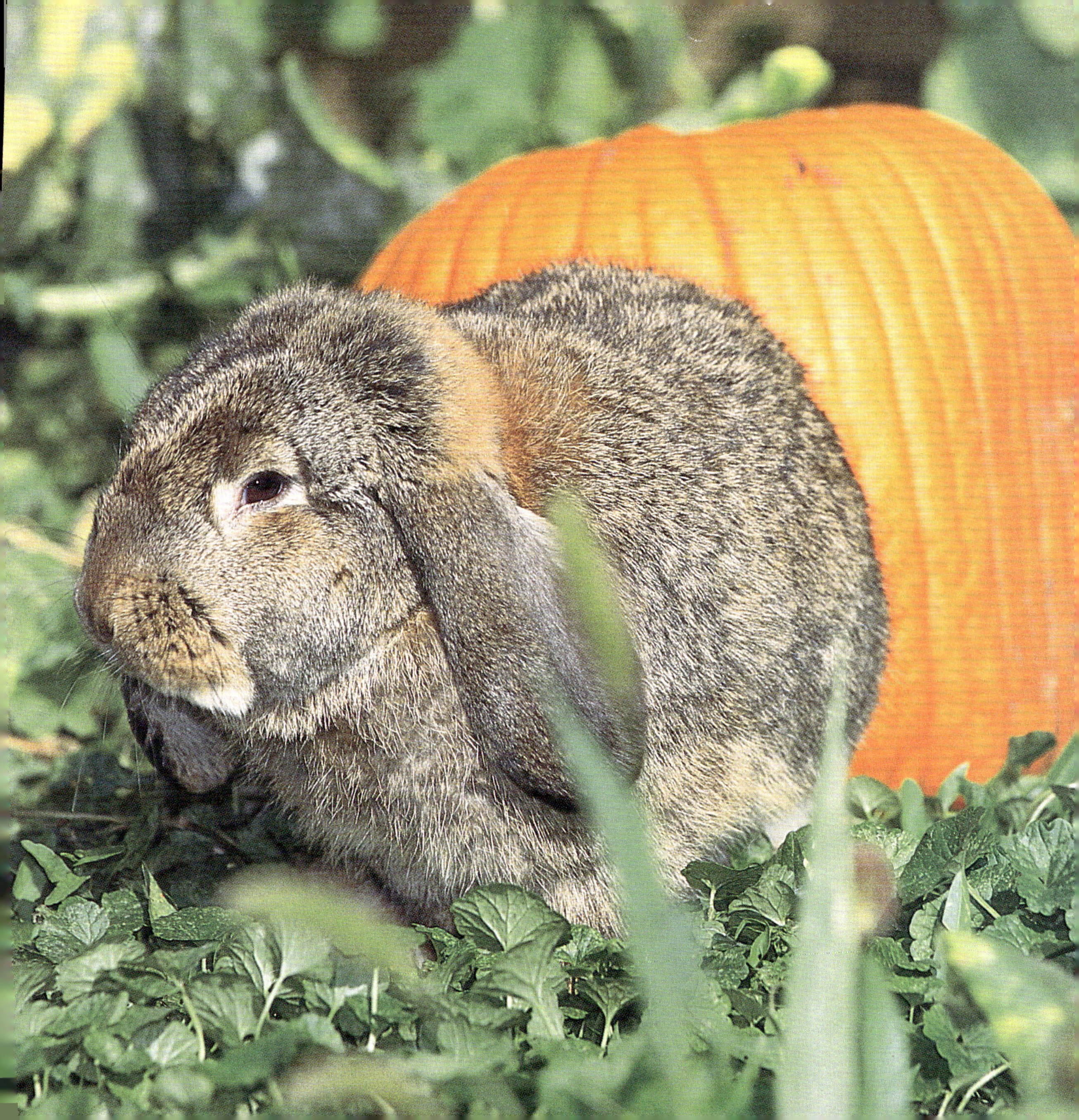

HOW RABBITS ARE USED

Farmers raise rabbits for many reasons. Some rabbits are raised for their tasty white meat. Rabbit fur is made into yarn, or used for gloves, coats and hats.

Many rabbits are sold as pets. They don't need much space, and they are clean and good-natured.

Some breeders exhibit, or show, rabbits at fairs and shows. The most important show is the American Rabbit Breeders Association National Convention.

Glossary

breed (BREED) — a special group or type of an animal, such as a *French lop* rabbit

breeder (BREED er) — a person who raises one or more breeds of domestic animals to sell or show

domestic (dum ES tihk) — referring to any of several kinds of animals tamed and raised by humans

hutch (HUTCH) — a rabbit's cage

lagomorph (LAG o morf) — a group of gnawing mammals, including rabbits, hares and pikas

litter (LIH ter) — an animal's newborn young, babies

rabbitry (RAH bih tree) — a place where domestic rabbits are raised; a rabbit farm

INDEX

American Rabbit Breeders
   Association National
   Convention   22
breeders   5, 11, 19, 22
dewlap   6
ears   6, 14
fairs   22
farmers   5
fur   22
gardens   5, 19
hares   14
hutches   9, 20
kits   16
lagomorphs   14
legs   6
meat   22
pets   22
rabbitries   5

rabbits
   age of   16
   breeds of   6, 11
   cottontail   14
   jack   14
   snowshoe   14
   weight of   6
   wild   5, 11, 14, 19, 20
shows   22

NORTH SMITHFIELD PUBLIC LIBRARY

3 5944 00067 8977

AUG 2001

DATE DUE

JUL 08 2017

DEMCO, INC. 38-2931